First Class Etiquette

From the Titanic to Now...Manners Matter

Penelope M. Carlevato
Illustrated by Amanda M. Carlevato

ISBN: 0692237542
ISBN 13: 9780692237540

A very special thank you to all my family and friends who have encouraged and supported me during the creation of this book. My English mother who taught me the art of hospitality and tea-time etiquette, and my husband, Norm, for never giving up on me and encouraging me to push on. A very special thank you to Amanda, my gifted granddaughter, who drew the illustrations for this book, and to my lifelong friend Beverly Athey for her poem, "Grandma and Me".

When I wrote the book *Tea on the Titanic,* I read and researched the history, customs, dress, and manners of that time, the Edwardian Era, around 1912. Since I have eleven grandchildren, I was interested in the manners and etiquette of children of that period. I found many social events, birthday parties, dinners, and afternoon teas recorded in numerous books. The accepted behavior, formalities, and menus of the right food to serve were written plainly for people to appreciate and observe. Many details of that era have not changed. Today, in the twenty-first century, it is still just as polite to have good manners and etiquette as it was on board the *Titanic* in 1912. The popular PBS television series *Downton Abbey* also gives us a peak into the manners and customs of that era.

My granddaughter Amanda helped me with this book by drawing the illustrations. Amanda is a twin. She loves to draw and loves to have tea. One day I was telling her about writing a book on etiquette and manners and we came up with the idea to work together. Since I was born in England and have been involved in the tea business for many years, naturally we thought it should be a tea book, but tea manners and etiquette are really the same as any table manners. Most of Amanda's drawings are of girls and boys who like to have tea.

We both feel that many young people, and adults too, lack the basics of good table manners. Our book is a fun guide for how to act when at the table eating a meal or having tea.

"Manners are a sensitive awareness of the feelings of others. If you have that awareness, you have good manners, no matter what fork you use." Emily Post

The Story of the Titanic

More than a hundred years ago, the most famous ship in history was the *Titanic*. It was built over three years in Belfast, Ireland, and was finished in 1912. It was the largest ship ever built at that time. The *Titanic* was longer than four football fields and weighed 46,000 tons. It could carry more than 3,200 people as passengers and crew, but the maiden voyage only had 2,208 on board.

The *Titanic* divided the passengers from the crew and cargo on ten different decks. Passengers were placed on seven decks, and the other three decks were for the crew and cargo. Passengers came from all over the world and from every level of society, divided into three classes: first class for the famous and wealthy, second class for the professional people, and third class for those who were coal miners, farmers, and shop workers, going to America to better their lives. In fact, most of the passengers were in third class, more than 700 men, women, and children.

The *Titanic* was one of the most beautiful ships ever built. In the first-class passenger areas, there were restaurants, lounges, a swimming pool, a gym, and fine staterooms. The food was wonderful in all three classes. The *Titanic's* maiden voyage was the first transatlantic sailing where passengers traveling in third class did not have to bring their own food or linens. Everyone traveled in style.

The *Titanic's* first voyage was in April of 1912. The ship left Southampton, England, for the week long journey to New York City. After four days crossing the Atlantic Ocean, it hit an iceberg. A great hole was slashed into the hull of the *Titanic,* and the ship began to fill up with ice-cold water. Many people did not think the ship was in danger and did not see the need to get into the lifeboats. The *Titanic* had only twenty lifeboats, which were not enough for all the people on board. The ship sank only two hours later, and many of the passengers drowned. Of the 2,208 passengers, only 706 survived.

Those people who did get in lifeboats were rescued by another ship, the *Carpathia,* which was more than four hours away. It received the SOS call and raced through iceberg- infested waters to reach the *Titanic* as quickly as it could.

The *Titanic* still lies over two and a half miles deep at the bottom of the ocean. Many of its items have been recovered from the wreck and are in museums all over the world.

Children of the Titanic

There were 133 children on the *Titanic*. Most children of that era, regardless of their social class, were respectful, obedient, and a credit to their families. Social status was reflected in children and was the reason why they were welcomed at the dinner or tea table. Many children from wealthy families had nannies, who were responsible for the upbringing and social training of children. No one knows for sure how many nannies were on the *Titanic*, but there were many families who could afford to travel with one.

Each class had mealtimes clearly spelled out.

The **first-class** children had their meals with their nannies, as it was highly unlikely that a child would stay awake for the many-course dinners served on the *Titanic* - sometimes as many as eleven courses, which typically began around seven or eight o'clock in the evening.

The **second-class** children might have their meals with their parents, as there may not have been a lot of nannies on board in this class. The children took their meals in the dining room at tables with white linen tablecloths and napkins, china dishes, and silver utensils (forks, knives, and spoons).

The **third-class** children ate their meals in the dining room with their families. Many of the families traveling in steerage, or third class, were on the way to a new life. Fathers had to find jobs and places to live, and the families needed to get used to a new way of life in America. Many of these families had never seen electric lights, running water, or flush toilets! The *Titanic* had all these things, and it was very exciting for the third-class passengers to have such nice accommodations.

When I was a little girl, our family traveled from the United States to England on a very large ocean liner, the SS United States, similar to the *Titanic*. It was the fastest ship in the world. We had a wonderful time, and we had to be on our best behavior. Before we left for our trip, we had many lessons on proper behavior while we were on board. One afternoon my mother and I were having afternoon tea on the ship with all the lovely dishes, teacups, white linen napkins, and dainty food. My mother said, "This must have been like it was on the *Titanic*." I asked her, "What is the *Titanic*?" She then told me the story, and that is how I first became interested in the *Titanic*.

This book will give you the information on manners and etiquette my parents insisted we know.

Manners

FIRST CLASS ALL THE WAY

Always knock before you enter.

It is always polite to announce yourself,
even if going into your brother's or sister's room.

Wash your hands before going to the table.

Hand washing is the number one way
to stay healthy and well.

Help set the table.

This helps Mom and gives you an advantage
when you are at a restaurant or a friend's house, as
you will know which silverware to use.

This is the correct way to place the items on the table.

To remember where to place the silverware,
remember the word "fork" has four letters,
and so does the word "left," so the fork goes on the left. The
word "knife" has five letters, just as the word "right," so the knife
goes on the right. A "spoon" has five letters and also goes next
to the knife. The sharp side of the knife goes next to the plate,
keeping the safe side out toward anyone sitting next to you.

Sit straight with feet on the floor.

(If your legs are long enough.)

Place your napkin on your lap.

A napkin is used for wiping your hands or your mouth at mealtime.
Don't ever blow your nose in your napkin.

Give thanks for your food.

Thank you for the food we eat,
Thank you for the world so sweet,
Thank you for the birds that sing,
Thank you, God, for everything.
Amen

Keep the teacup and saucer on the table while pouring the hot tea.

If you try to pour tea while holding a cup and saucer in your hand, you might splash hot tea on your fingers.

Pour the tea for your guests.

Do not pass the teapot around the table.

Ask for food to be passed, instead of reaching across the table for food.

The correct way to pass food around the table is to give the serving plate to the person on your right.

Say "please" and "thank you" when food is passed.

First-class manners for everyone!

Chew with your mouth closed.

Nobody else wants to see what you are eating.

Keep elbows and other body parts off the table.

There's not room on the table for feet, knees, and food.

Engage in conversations with everyone at the table.

Everyone should be included in the table talk.

No cell phones or texting while at the table.

Turn off your phone and enjoy your friends, family, and food.
No one wants an "app" for mealtime.

Always thank the person who made the meal – Mom included!

Have an attitude of gratitude. There is always something to be thankful for.

Ask to be excused when finished.

Always say "excuse me" whenever you leave the table.

You don't have to tell the reason!

Tea Party Etiquette

A Tea Party

A tea party is a small meal usually served in the afternoon that has tea, little crustless sandwiches, scones, cakes, and cookies.

Special Manners at the Tea Table

* You may eat the tea sandwiches with your fingers, but take small bites. Don't shove the whole sandwich in your mouth.

* When eating scones, break off a small piece, then place a small amount of jam and clotted cream on the scone. Another way to eat a scone is to cut it in half like a hamburger bun, then put the jam and cream on each half, but don't put the two halves back together. The *clotted cream is only for the scone, not for the tea.

Clotted Cream - In England, cow's milk from several areas is made into a lovely, thick cream, almost like butter. It can be purchased in the United States at specialty stores in glass jars. It can be called clotted cream, Devonshire cream, or Cornish cream. You can make something similar using whipping cream. Recipe on page 36.

* Always use sugar tongs (not your fingers) to remove the
  sugar cube from the sugar bowl to your teacup.

* When putting sugar cubes into your teacup, do it before the tea is poured,
  so the tea won't splash out of your cup and the sugar tongs won't get wet.

* Use milk in your tea, never half-and-half, cream, or coffee flavors.

* Stir the milk, sugar, or both in your tea very quietly, not hitting the side
  of the cup with the spoon. You may also use honey to sweeten your tea.

* If the tea is very hot, wait a few minutes for it to cool down.

* Hold the teacup normally. Don't extend your little finger.

* Don't gulp your tea. Sip it slowly.

* Always remove your spoon from the teacup and
  place it behind the teacup on the saucer.

* When drinking your tea, look at your guests and not into the teacup.

* If you are offered lemon slices for your tea, never add milk
  too! (The milk will curdle and leave little gross chunks.)

It's Time for a Tea Party

Planning and Serving

Oh, what a fun time we can have by inviting friends, boys and girls, to come to your home for a tea party! Choose a time that is convenient for your friends, and especially Mom or Grandma, so they will be available to help. One of my favorite teatimes is with my grandchildren. Ask your grandmother to have a tea party with you. You will both have a tea-rific time.

Grandma and Me

Off we went
Just Grandma and me
To celebrate a cup
Of tea.

We walked to town
And there it was
The Little Tea Room
Just for us.

Grandma asked me
Not to stare
At all the ladies
Seated there.

The tea was poured
And to my surprise
It danced around
Before my eyes.

The sandwiches and
Scones we shared
I thought how much
My Grandma cared.

To take me off to
Tea that day,
We let the time
Just pass away.

The memories now
Still linger near,
That day that was
So very dear.

Beverly Ann Mortensen Athey

Planning your tea party

* Start by setting a date and time (afternoon is best.)
  Saturday or Sunday afternoons about two or three o'clock
  is a great time. Tell your friends that this is a special time to
  dress up. Encourage the girls to wear hats and gloves.

* Make some pretty invitations. Use construction paper to cut out a
  shape of a teapot and cover it with a paper doily. Write the date and
  time with gel pens. Use stickers, ribbons, and glitter to decorate.

Where
When
Time
Occasion (Birthday?)
Phone number
Address
Dress

RSVP

(Go here http://FirstClassEtiquette.com/invitation to
print a large size teapot as an invitation)

* A few weeks before the tea, send out the invitations and make
  sure everyone knows he or she needs to let you know if he or
  she can come or not. That is what "RSVP" stands for. (In French,
  repondez, s'il vous plait - meaning "Please respond!")

* Now comes the fun part! Planning your menu and
  shopping for the food. Use the following recipes to serve
  up a delicious assortment of treats and sweets.

A Titanic Tea Party

Recipes
The order for serving at a tea:

TEA SANDWICHES

SCONES

SWEETS

Tea Sandwiches

CURRIED CHICKEN TEA SANDWICHES

2 cups white chicken meat (canned is OK)

¼ cup mayonnaise

2 green onions (finely chopped)

¼ cup chopped cashews

½ teaspoon curry powder

Butter (room temperature)

Bread (freeze the loaf of bread first
as it will be easier to make the sandwiches)

1. Ask an adult to cut the chicken into small pieces

2. Mix together the chicken, mayonnaise, onions, cashews, and curry powder.

3. Spread the mixture onto the buttered bread.

4. Trim the crusts from the bread and cut the sandwiches into desired shapes.

5. Keep the sandwiches covered with a damp paper towel until ready to serve.

Cucumber Tea Sandwiches

1 English Hothouse cucumber

Cream cheese, softened

Dill weed

Bread (freeze the loaf of bread first
as it will be easier to make the sandwiches)

1. Ask an adult to slice the cucumber into very thin slices.
2. Place the cucumber slices on paper towels to help absorb some of the liquid from the cucumber.
3. Spread the cream cheese onto the bread slices.
4. Place the cucumber slices on top of the cream cheese on half of the bread slices, overlapping slightly.
5. Sprinkle the cucumbers lightly with dill weed.
6. Top with the other bread slices that have been spread with the cream cheese.
7. Trim the crusts and cut the sandwiches into desired shapes.

Other sandwiches to try: egg salad, peanut butter and jelly, cheese and tomato, and turkey.

Scones

You may purchase scones at any bakery, or use a mix that is easy to bake. If you want to bake the scones, here is a yummy recipe. Always have an adult help you, especially turning on the oven and putting the baking sheet in and taking it out of the oven.

ORANGE CRANBERRY SCONES

2 cups flour

2 teaspoons sugar

1 teaspoon cream of tartar

1 teaspoon baking soda

½ teaspoon salt

½ cup butter

¾ cup orange juice

¼ cup dried cranberries

1. Sift together the first 5 ingredients.
2. *Cut into the dry ingredients the butter, add the cranberries, and then stir in the orange juice. (Less handling of the dough makes fluffier scones.) *Cutting the butter into the flour mixture means to mix them together using a pastry blender or two knives until they resemble little crumbs.
3. Divide dough into 2 portions, then pat into rounds ¾-inch thick, and cut into eight equal sized wedges, but do not separate, or cut into rounds with a floured cookie cutter. Place scones on lightly greased or parchment-lined baking sheet.
4. Bake 12 to 15 minutes at 400°F.
5. Serve warm with jam and cream - Devonshire cream, clotted cream, or mock-Devonshire cream.

MOCK DEVONSHIRE CREAM

Serve the scones with this mock-Devonshire cream.

1 drop yellow food coloring
1 cup heavy whipping cream
¼ cup sour cream

1. Add the food coloring to the whipping cream
2. Beat the cream with an electric mixer until very stiff.
3. Gradually blend in sour cream.
4. Serve with strawberry or raspberry jam to go with each piece of your scone that you break off.

Sweets

EASY BERRY TARTS

Strawberries, raspberries or blueberries,
washed and hulled

Prepackaged tart shells

Whipped cream or topping

1. Place berries in tart shells.
2. Top with whipped cream.

OREO COOKIE

This would be fun to serve, as the Oreo was a brand new cookie in America in 1912!

SHORTBREAD COOKIES

1 cup butter, softened

½ cup sugar

2 cups all-purpose flour, sifted

Using an electric mixer, beat together the butter and sugar until creamy. Gradually work in the flour with your hands until you have a smooth, stick-together ball of dough. On a lightly floured surface, knead well (squeeze together with your hands) to a smooth dough and roll out to 1/2-inch thick. Cut the dough into finger-size pieces or use a cookie cutter. Place on an ungreased baking sheet and prick the top of the cookies with a fork. Bake at 350°F for about 15 to 20 minutes, until very pale golden. Leave cookies on the baking sheet for 1 minute to cool, then transfer to a wire rack and sprinkle with sugar while still warm. Store in an airtight container when cool. Don't over bake; cookies are done when pale golden, and tops will feel dry. Always have an adult help you when putting cookies in and taking them out of the hot oven.

It's almost tea time!

Preparing the proper cup of tea.

Tea Bags (Earl Grey or English breakfast are good choices)

Milk

Sugar Cubes

1. Always ask an adult to bring fresh cold water to a boil in a teakettle.

2. Warm a teapot with hot water from the faucet. When the water in the teakettle comes to a boil, pour out the warm water that was in the teapot.

3. Place the tea bags in the teapot and pour the boiling water over the tea bags.

4. Let the tea set for three to five minutes, then use a spoon to carefully remove the tea bags. Leaving the tea bags in the water for a longer time will cause your tea to be bitter, not stronger.

5. Place the milk and sugar cubes in the teacups, and pour the tea into each cup.

SETTING THE TABLE

Cover the table with a pretty tablecloth or placemats, then set the table with teacups, plates, napkins, spoons, forks, and a small knife. You won't need a soup spoon, dinner knife, or dinner fork. For a special touch, add a vase of fresh flowers. Follow the diagram for setting the table.

Now you are ready for your tea party!

Titanic Princess Tea Party

Miss Jamie and friends

I am honored to be able to attend a wonderful Princess Tea Party at the Titanic Museum in Pigeon Forge, Tennessee, every May. Up to five hundred little girls come to this event. Each guest is given a lesson on manners and etiquette by the *Titanic's* first-class maid, Miss Jamie. She teaches correct table setting, serving etiquette, and the very proper way to eat finger sandwiches and cookies, and how to prepare and drink tea. It is a wonderful time for all the children and parents who come. Every little girl leaves the tea party with her own teacup and a new special awareness of being a princess. You may not be able to attend this fun event, but have Mom check the local papers in your area for teas for children and etiquette classes.

To find teacups and saucers, teapots, and other things for your tea parties, it's always fun to go to garage sales and thrift shops. Also think about asking your grandmother, aunts, or friends if they have teacups they are not using.

One of my favorite places to buy lovely tea (and anything else you need for your tea party) is www.AnniesTeaTime.com (Annie will send everything you need for your party in the mail).

Amanda and I hope you had fun reading our book. We would love to hear from you. Let us know about your tea parties.

Email us at: Penelopesteatime@gmail.com

*Come and visit us at our book signings when we are at the Titanic Museum in Pigeon Forge, TN. Please check the following web sites for dates and times of this and other book signings and teas. We would love to meet you.

www.FirstClassEtiquette.com or www.TitanicPigeonForge.com

More recipes and tea party ideas are at our website:
www.FirstClassEtiquette.com

"Treat others the way you would want to be treated."
The Book of Proverbs

Made in the USA
San Bernardino, CA
09 September 2016